the guide to owning a
FERRET

Mary Field

T.F.H. Publications, Inc.
One TFH Plaza
Third and Union Avenues
Neptune City, NJ 07753

This book has been published with the intent to provide accurate and authoritative information in regard to the subject matter within. While every precaution has been taken in preparation of this book, the publisher and author assume no responsibility for errors or omissions. Neither is any liability assumed for damages resulting from the use of the information herein.

ISBN 0-7938-2151-7

Contents

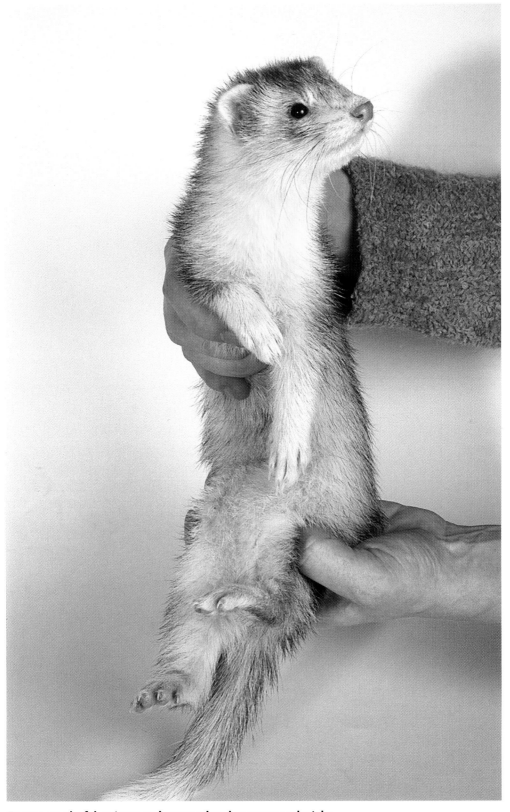

Ferrets are playful, quiet pets that are related to otters and minks.

THE GUIDE TO OWNING A FERRET

Introduction

It is doubtful that a book on domestic ferrets would have been published, much less purchased, 30 years ago. Although pet ferrets have been around since the days of the ancient Egyptians, it wasn't until the 1980s that they became vastly popular as a pet, and were no longer considered a "dangerous exotic."

In 3000 B.C., ferrets were domesticated by the Egyptians. Domestic ferrets were bred with the European polecat and introduced by the Crusaders of the 10th century to Europe as working ferrets. Ferrets came to the US in the 1700s on ships from Europe to be used for rodent control. Ferrets would be released in barns or granaries to chase rats out of hiding places.

The Ferret Fanciers Club has over 3000 members. Many people all over the world keep ferrets as pets.

In England and some European countries, ferrets are still being used for hunting purposes, as well as being domesticated for pets. The use of hunting ferrets in the US is illegal. It is not surprising that domestic ferrets are now very popular pets. These little animals have become the pride and joy of their loving owners.

Although they combine many of the best qualities of dogs and cats, they are still unique entities. They are quiet, clean, litter-trainable, small enough to fit in any size house or apartment, forever playful, extremely inquisitive and mischievous enough to be constantly entertaining pets. However, they are only pets. Their owners purchase them solely to love and enjoy (okay, spoil and pamper) and that they do! Many people who are allergic to dogs and/or cats have not found this to be a problem with ferrets. The only thing more enjoyable as a pet than a ferret is two or more!

It is difficult to give an exact figure of the number of pet ferrets in the US, since licensing of ferrets is not required in most areas. Also, ferret owners in states and districts that ban ferrets are understandably reluctant to "stand up and be counted."

When my late husband, Jay, and I purchased our first ferret, Furry, in 1984, there was virtually no information on ferret care. We were curious to read about ferrets and to network with other ferret owners. For that reason we started the Ferret Fanciers Club (FFC) in 1985, which has grown to more than 3000 members around the world. Over the years our mail and phone calls relate to many, many subjects. In this book we will discuss the problems and concerns over which ferret owners have turned to us for advice.

Ferrets, a member of the family Mustelidae, are related to the otter, weasel, mink, marten, ermine, badger, and skunk and are cousins of the black-footed ferret. In the 1980s, the black-footed ferret was nearly extinct, with only six survivors existing; however, the tribe is now increasing and, hopefully someday, will no longer be on the endangered species list.

Ferrets range in size from less than one pound to five pounds. Neutered or spayed ferrets are smaller and females usually weigh up to one pound less than males.

An average, neutered male weighs approximately two to three pounds.

Males are called "hobs," females "jills," and young ferrets "kits."

Is a Ferret Right for you?

We urge you to consider this matter seriously. Ferrets have a life span of eight to ten years and need attention and affection. If you fall in love with an adorable ferret in a pet store, we hope you will resist the impulse to bring him home until you have thought it out. Taking a ferret into your home requires a commitment to prepare for it, offer it love, and give it the best of care. It should not be done on a whim, but only after careful consideration and agreement of all living in the household.

While ferrets are ideal pets for most people, there are some households that should not have ferrets or should defer the purchase. Because ferrets are so small, they are not ideal pets for the less agile individual. We also strongly urge that ferrets (or any domestic animal) not be left unattended with children under the age of six. If you travel away from home frequently, consider who will take care of your pet. If you can't spend several hours a day giving love and companionship to a ferret, it is unfair to adopt one, since they thrive on attention.

NO PETS ALLOWED

If you live in a rented house or apartment

Ferrets are inquisitive and intelligent pets that require a lot of attention from their owners.

with a "no-pet" clause, you still might be able to have the joy of the companionship of a ferret. Many landlords have the no-pet clause in the lease to save the trouble of dealing with tenants owning pets on an individual basis. If nobody is allowed to have a pet, that's one less hassle for the landlord to contend with. Certainly a landlord might be justified in not wanting a 125-pound dog in a 3-room apartment, but by declaring "no pets allowed" such pets as clean, quiet ferrets are excluded.

When hunting for a rental house or apartment, take a picture of your ferret. It's hard to refuse permission to have such a small, quiet pet. If the landlord verbally agrees that you can have your ferret, get it in writing in your lease.

If you live in a house or apartment where pets have been banned, lawyers interested in animal rights and the rights of pet owners offer the following advice: "Don't automatically give up your pet...no-pet clause or not, it is possible to win in court. A good lawyer can often find careless wording in a lease that renders the no-pet clause legally unenforceable."

Please read this book through before going any further with ferret adoption. It may answer many questions and help you make a final decision.

OTHER PETS

We receive many questions regarding adding a ferret to a home that has a dog or cat. Our advice is to introduce the animals to each other gradually. Never leave the two animals unattended until you are positive that they get along well. Although ferrets are quick and hide in small places, they are extremely small and can be seriously injured or killed by a dog or cat. Since their instinct is to pursue rabbits, rabbits and ferrets usually are not a good mix. A recent survey of our members disclosed that more than 90 percent of ferret owners also own other pets.

It is advisable to let your ferret have a couple of days to adjust to his new home before being exposed to other pets. When introduction time comes, take a towel that your ferret has used as bedding and give it to your other pet. Take some bedding from that pet and place it in your ferret's cage. This will provide an advance introduction. The next day, take your ferret and other pet to "neutral territory"—neither near the ferret's cage nor your other pet's sleeping or eating area. Give both pets suitable treats and talk softly and lovingly to them while giving pats. This will let the pets know that when they are together, pleasurable things will happen. Keep them together only a short time. Build up to longer periods of time together, always under supervision. **Never** leave the animals alone until you are 100 percent certain that they will get along.

Preparing for Your Ferret's Homecoming

Before you go shopping for your ferret, you **must** ready a "layette." A starter kit for ferrets must include; small, heavy dishes for food and water (to prevent tipping and spilling). An alternative would be a water bottle attached to the side of

Although fun to play in, houseplants can be hazardous to your ferret. Keep him away from plants that could be poisonous.

the cage. These bottles are good because the water is kept clean and always available. The bottles also prevent the bedding from becoming wet.

FERRET CAGES

Even if you plan to allow your ferret the run of the house, it is advisable to purchase a cage. Although ferrets love to roam, litter training is easier in a cage, and your little pet will be safer in a cage when you are out of the house or asleep.

The dimensions should be no less than 36 by 24 by 18 inches to house one or two ferrets; if there are more than two ferrets in the same cage, it should be proportionally larger. Wire is recommended because it is easy to clean and does not absorb odors. Glass aquariums or plastic cages should not be used, as they do not provide enough ventilation. However, be sure the floor is covered with soft toweling or indoor/outdoor (washable) carpet to prevent their feet from damage by the wire. Be sure the wire grids are close enough together so the ferret does not escape. There should be no sharp wires exposed.

One very good type of cage is the "two-story" style with a ramp connecting the two levels. On the bottom level the litter pan and food can be stored, leaving enough room for the ferret. The top level is also for the ferret to roam, and they have great fun going up and down the ramp. Always provide lots of clean towels for the ferrets to curl up in at naptime.

The litter pan should be of plastic with sides low enough for the ferret to get in and out easily. A good grade of cat litter (not newspaper or cedar shavings) should fill the pan about one-quarter full.

When you purchase your pet, ask what he has been eating. Adjusting to a new home will be easier with familiar food. We'll discuss weaning from one food to another later.

FERRET SAFETY

It is a good idea to keep a collar on your ferret at all times. We found that a small bell will help you keep tabs on the little rascal, and if your ferret strays, a collar will let everyone know that this is a pet.

If you haven't had a chance to observe a ferret closely you'll be amazed at the tiny spaces they can get into—it's almost as if they were made of moldable rubber. Decide what areas your ferret can roam in. Then, armed with cardboard or plywood and duct tape, ferret-proof these areas. Cover any entrances to the area under the stove, behind the refrigerator, or any other unmovable items. Check window screens, areas under doors, air ducts, etc. Ferrets are great climbers and will crawl up curtains, screens, or any material that will afford a good grasp. Remove or cover all electrical wires at floor level to prevent the ferret from chewing them. Lock up all toxic substances and keep the toilet lid down.

Houseplants can also cause poisoning—keep them away from your ferret. Also, ferrets love to dig in the dirt around the plant. To prevent problems, put a few ferret droppings in the plant. They are odorless but will discourage ferret visits.

A wire cage is recommended for ferrets because it is easy to clean and does not absorb odors. Make sure that there are no sharp edges exposed. The bottom of the cage should be covered with outdoor carpeting or a towel to protect the ferret's feet.

Surprisingly, our Furry got through a hole in the wall that was meant for an electrical plug—since it was not used and behind our stereo, there was no plate on it. We spent nearly an hour trying to coax him out by offering him raisins (his favorite treat). Incidentally, the reason he wanted to "leave home" was because the day before we had acquired Heather, a female ferret we rescued from an abusive and neglectful home. Although in time they became inseparable, the beginning was rough. He felt threatened by her presence and she, having been so abused, mistrusted everyone and everything. It took several months before she became the dear, gentle, affectionate ferret she now is.

Don't forget to check out mail slots and be sure the ferret has no access to a clothes dryer or a reclining chair. If snoozing inside the chair, a ferret could be fatally crushed if the chair is pushed in a reclining position or upright position.

Be sure cleaning products, floor wax, shoe polish, drain cleaners, household bleach, mothballs, and rodent control products are out of reach. Bathtubs with even one inch of water are also a potential danger.

FERRET LAWS

This is a good time to check your state and local regulations. At the time of printing, ferrets are illegal in several states. The FFC is working to legalize ferrets in all states, and we have been able to make some progress since 1985. Hopefully, soon there will be no restrictions in all 50 states. Many cities require licensing or permits for keeping ferrets. Check with your local authorities about the legality of keeping these pets. If ferret-keeping is illegal in your state, consider getting another pet.

Selecting Your Ferret

Ready to go ferret shopping? The FFC receives many phone calls asking us to recommend breeders. Presently we do not have a list of approved breeders for retail sale. This is not to suggest retail breeders are not acceptable; we can't check these facilities out and we don't make recommendations on facilities, services, or products we can't personally investigate. Our suggestion is to go to a pet shop. If they do not have ferrets, they can order them.

The pet shop should be reputable and offer a guarantee. The ferrets offered for sale should be "pet quality" which means the ferrets have been raised with

When selecting your new pet, choose a ferret that is attentive, alert, and healthy. A reputable pet shop will allow you to examine the ferret closely.

Healthy ferrets have short legs that are heavily boned. Their paws should we well-furred between the pads. The fur should be soft with a sheen and there should be no scaly or bald patches on the ferret's body.

abundant social interaction from the age of three weeks on. In large ferret breeding operations, teenagers are hired to actively socialize the young ferrets prior to shipment to pet shops. If socialization is not done, the ferrets will relate to humans as they do their littermates—by biting.

Many of our members advertise through the *International Ferret Review,* the FFC newsletter. We suggest you also watch the classified ads in your paper— frequently there are ferret kits or adults for sale. Your veterinarian can be a good source of available ferrets too. Many animal shelters have abandoned ferrets awaiting a good home.

Although all ferrets look adorable, be sure to let your head guide your heart when making your choice. Healthy ferrets should exhibit inquisitive behavior with no lethargy or listlessness. Since they sleep so soundly, they may be a bit listless if they are awakened but should "spring into action" quickly.

Fur should be soft with a sheen. There should be no bald or scaly patches.

Check the teeth for chips or breaks. Bottom teeth should fit firmly behind the upper canines. Teeth should be clean and white (no discoloration) and unbroken. None should be missing. The gums should be pink.

Heads of males are rounder and broader than those of females, which are smaller with a longer tapering towards the nose. Whiskers should be long and full.

Eyes should be bright with little or no discharge accumulated in the corners.

Ears should be clean. If the ferret is continually scratching the ears or shaking the head, suspect ear mites.

The nose should be moist if the ferret is awake. If he has been sleeping, it may be dry because the ferret will nuzzle in bedding material. The nose should not be cracked or scaly.

The neck should be strong and muscular without folds or laps. There should not be any narrowing of the neck at the head or shoulders.

Rapid heaving of the chest may mean lung or heart problems. The abdomen should not be swollen.

Body should be slightly elongated with smooth lines when still. In motion, body should be rounded without showing any sharp or flat angles. There are basically two body types—"whippet" and "bulldog." The bulldog type has short, thick legs and neck, a blunt, broad face, and a wide chest. The whippet is fine boned, leggy, and lanky, with a more pointed head and arched back.

Examine the skin for hair loss, bumps, or scabs.

If the vulva is swollen, it is a sign the female was not spayed or is exhibiting signs of Cushing's disease. Swollen, hard glands on either side of the anus in both sexes is a symptom of blockage of these glands.

Kits and non-breeding ferrets usually lack a distinctive mask.

The tail should be straight without curvature and have a thick base tapering to the tip. It should be fully furred. Tail

Ferrets are being bred in many fur colors. This ferret is a Chocolate-Point.

length should not exceed one-third the ferret's length.

Legs should be short, heavy in bone, and strong.

Paws should be well-furred between the pads. The paw shape should be oval and show no splaying between the toes. Pads and webbing should be free of cracks and scales.

Surface color should conform to coat color. The lighter the coat, the lighter the nose.

Even though your ferret has been spayed or neutered and descented, there will probably be more of an odor about this pet than you would like. This is because he has been communally living with other ferrets in the pet store. A bath should take care of this problem.

Usually pet shops will offer neutered or spayed ferrets only. This is good, since an unneutered male can have a strong, pungent odor and be a more aggressive pet. Also, there are many difficulties with breeding a female ferret.

Often the ferrets are descented at the same time that they are neutered, but if they haven't been it is not really a problem. Bathing and general cleanliness will take care of the odor problem. On a rare occasion, if the ferret becomes frightened or upset he will emit a strong odor, but this is very infrequent and the odor soon dissipates.

There is no difference in temperament between a neutered male and a spayed

The coat color of the ferret you choose is a personal preference. It makes no difference in the animal's temperament.

female. Ferrets come in a wide variety of colors, including:

Siamese—light colored animal with legs, mask, and tail showing darker complimentary color. Guardhairs should allow undercoat to show clearly.

Sable Point—undercoat white to cream. Guard hairs and points dark brown. Nose and pad leather brick red to brown. Eyes as black as possible.

White-Footed Sable—same as Sable Point, but has four white feet and a white throat patch and usually a black nose.

Chocolate Point—undercoat white to cream, points and guard hairs milk chocolate. Nose leather pink to brown—often mottled, pad leather pink to brown. Eyes brown.

Butterscotch—undercoat same as Sable. Guard hairs and points are butterscotch vs. black. Nose also butterscotch. Whitefooted Butterscotch has four white feet and white throat patch. Eyes brown.

Blue Point—undercoat white to blue-white, guard hairs and points slate blue. Nose and pad leather slate to lavender (slate preferred), eyes brown.

Red Point—undercoat white to buff, points and guard hairs from red to rust to reddish brown. Nose and pad leather coral to brick, eyes brown.

Cinnamon—undercoat white or off-white. Guard hairs reddish brown (cinnamon). Nose and pad leather pink to brick. Eyes brown.

Lilac—undercoat white to blue-white, points pinkish or lavender gray. Nose and pad leather pink to lavender. Eyes brown.

Self Coloration—an even color over entire body.

Onyx-Eyed White—solid white with black eyes. Sexually mature adults may have a yellowish cast. Red nose and pad leather pink.

Ruby-Eyed White—solid white, red eyes. Sexually mature adults may have a reddish tinge. Red nose and pad leather pink.

Black Self—solid black, no mask or markings. Nose and pad leather black. Eyes black.

Blue Self—solid slate blue, nose and pad leather slate to lavender. Eyes brown.

Red—undercoat buff to orange. Points and guard hairs orange to red. Nose and pad leather coral to brick. Eyes brown.

Mauve—undercoat white to cream. Points and guard hairs pinkish tan. Nose and pad leather pink to mauve. Eyes brown.

Silver—undercoat white to cream. Points silver to silvery tan, guardhairs tipped with gray. Nose and pad leather pink to pinkish tan. Eyes brown.

Bi-Color—any color and white distributed in a 50/50 ratio.

Silver Mitt—any color except albino or white. May have white paws, body markings, shields, tipped tails.

The coloration of your chosen ferret is purely a personal preference; it makes no difference in the temperament of the ferret.

Be sure to ask what your ferret has been eating. Purchase some of that food and feed only that for a few days until your new pet feels at home. There are many good ferret foods on the market, or a good kitten (not cat) chow is also acceptable temporarily. If you want to wean your pet from the food he has been eating, do it gradually. Once your ferret starts to feel at home, mix a small amount of the new food with the old brand. Each day, increase the amount of new food and decrease the old. In about five days the ferret should be eating only the new brand.

Bringing Your Ferret Home

Be sure at least two people go to purchase the ferret—one person can hold the new addition to the household in his carrier while the other drives. Bring a small cardboard box filled with crushed paper towels for the ferret to travel in. Of course, the top of the box should have holes for adequate ventilation. If you have a pet carrier, this is ideal.

When you arrive home with the new ferret, let him explore the cage. He will probably be ready for a nap (it's surprising how much sleep these little pets require). Upon awakening, be sure he visits the litter pan. After sleep, ferrets relieve themselves. If you find him looking around a bit puzzled, gently pick him up and place him in the pan. After the desired results, lavishly praise your little pet.

You can now enjoy a play period. For the first few days, the ferret will probably spend lots of time exploring the ferret-proofed room. Be sure to spend lots of time with your new pet, giving plenty of cuddles and soft-spoken conversation. This will reassure your ferret and help him relate to you.

Young ferrets, like puppies, do bite. This is how they play with their littermates and they mean nothing personal by it. However, their sharp teeth hurt. It is best to stop this biting habit as early as possible. Your behavior can also influence biting habits. Teasing or rough play, running or screeching will encourage biting. Don't tease or play roughly with your new ferret. When you are bitten say, "NO!" in a firm and loud voice, tap the ferret on the nose (gently—this is just a little animal), and return the ferret to the cage for ten minutes. Do this immediately and consistently and the ferret will quickly get the message. If the biting continues, spray some biting deterrent in the ferret's face. It won't harm him, but he will hate the odor.

Set up the cage before you bring your ferret home. This will make his transition into your home less stressful.

Once you acquire your new pet, find a veterinarian who treats ferrets. Now is a good time to make sure your ferret has all the necessary inoculations.

If your pet chews on furniture or other items that shouldn't be bitten, spray these with the biting deterrent frequently. Also, be sure to provide hard rubber toys for chewing. Remember, with proper training at the start, in time ferrets outgrow the biting stage just as puppies do.

Gradually, you may wish to add to the rooms where your ferret is welcome. Just be sure to thoroughly ferret-proof these areas.

Within a week after acquiring your ferret we urge you to find a veterinarian who treats ferrets. Take in your new pet for his inoculations and a check-up. Don't wait for an emergency to locate a veterinarian. It is best for your veterinarian to get acquainted with your pet while he is healthy. This permits the examination to be more leisurely and, by knowing your pet when he is healthy, will enable the doctor to observe unusual symptoms if they occur. Just to be safe, also locate a 24-hour emergency clinic if this service is not provided by your veterinarian. If you have trouble locating a veterinarian experienced with ferrets in your area, contact a ferret club, either locally or via the Internet, for suggestions.

Housing

Domestic ferrets can live outdoors, but they are so small it really is no problem keeping them inside. Indoor ferrets are more affectionate and human-oriented if kept with their owners. You'll miss much of their adorable antics and they will be less of a pet if they are kept outdoors.

A heavy food bowl that cannot be tipped over is recommended. Empty and clean out the dish once a day.

It is a good idea to buy a cage for safety and training purposes. Remember, ferrets are so small that a cage seems like quite a bit of room to them. However, be sure they have several hours of freedom daily for play, human companionship, and exercise.

Ferrets cannot withstand extremes in temperature. They suffer greatly if the temperature is much above 80 degrees. Never put their cages in a draft or where direct sun is shining on them. Even if the room temperature is comfortable, the direct sun will heat them up. Also, be sure their cage is not receiving a blast from the heating or air conditioning duct.

The best bedding is soft towels fluffed up so they can cuddle up in them. Some ferrets will chew up the towels, if your ferret does, watch him closely to see if he becomes ill. Ferrets love to hide to sleep, so let them disappear in their bedding for a snooze.

The cage should be cleaned weekly using water and a mild detergent. Scrub, rinse, and cover surfaces with a disinfectant. Leave the disinfectant on for ten minutes, then rinse well. The bedding should be changed weekly—more often if there has been an accident.

Food bowls should be emptied of uneaten food daily, wiped clean, and refilled. Wash bowls in dish detergent at least every week. Don't fill the food bowl completely, because some ferrets will not eat stale food.

Water bottles should be emptied, cleaned with dish detergent, thoroughly rinsed, and refilled daily. A soft toothbrush or bottle brush is good for cleaning inside. Be sure to clean the rubber stopper and drinking tube.

Litter Training

Ferrets are very clean animals by nature and will not want to soil the areas in which they live. For this reason, they will be litter-trained more quickly if caged.

Put the litter box on the opposite side of the cage from the food. The litter box should be plastic (for easy cleaning) and filled one-fourth full of a good, non-

Ferrets are clean, neat animals and can be easily trained to use a litter box. The box should be plastic for easy cleaning and low enough for the ferret to climb into.

clumping cat litter. Once the ferret has used the box, leave the droppings in. When the litter is changed, take away most of the soiled litter, leaving just a bit to mix with the fresh litter. That way the ferret will remember the purpose of the box and will be discouraged from using it to play in.

If your ferret refuses to use the box except when he is placed in it, you might want to try changing litter brands. Be sure the litter box is kept clean by daily maintenance—ferrets are fastidious animals and will be "turned off" by an unclean litter box.

When pouring the litter from the bag, you may see some dust rise. This dust can cause problems if the ferret inhales it. Always pour litter in an area away from your pet. Sprinkle a few drops of water over the fresh litter and allow it to settle before putting it down for use. If your ferret pushes the box around the cage, you may need to add weight to it.

When out of the cage, ferrets seem to choose their favorite corner for a bathroom. We have found it easier to accommodate them by placing litter boxes in the corners they choose. If the room in which they can run is large, more than one litter box is the answer. A little patience is necessary.

If an "accident" should occur, clean the spot thoroughly to remove all odor so misbehavior won't become a habit. If a spot is left on the carpet, a good removal method is: mix one part white vinegar, one part water, and one-fourth part powdered laundry detergent. Mix well and apply with clean white cloth to spot. Pat over spot. Rinse with clear, cool water and allow to dry. Repeat these steps if necessary. Test this solution on a hidden part of the carpet first.

If your ferret makes a mistake, it is pointless to punish him by rubbing his nose in the feces. If your ferret absolutely refuses to use any other litter box but that in the cage, simply don't permit him to leave the cage until he has used the box.

Grooming

You will find that ferrets require relatively little grooming compared with most dogs. They usually need a bath once or twice a month. Unless they have been outdoors and gotten unusually dirty, try not to bathe them more often, as bathing can dry the skin. Some ferrets love bath time, some tolerate it, and to some it's the worst thing ever invented. To bathe your ferret, put a small amount of

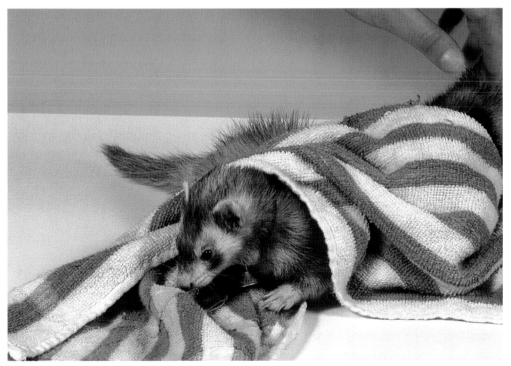

After a bath, be sure to dry your ferret thoroughly. He may want to dry himself off in a fluffy towel.

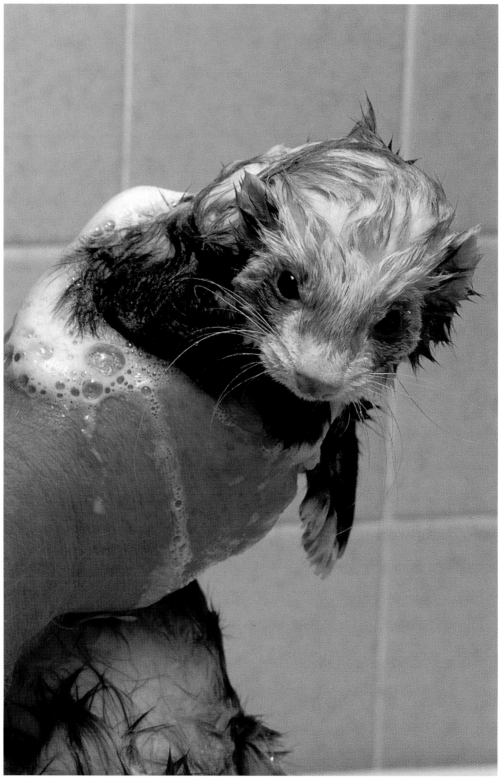

Ferrets usually need a bath once or twice a month. Some ferrets love bath time and enjoy playing in the water.

THE GUIDE TO OWNING A FERRET

lukewarm water in a small sink (we use the kitchen sink). While talking softly to your ferret, be sure he is thoroughly wet. Then, using a special ferret shampoo (available at pet stores), gently rub the body. Rinse thoroughly, including the face, being careful not to get water up the nose. If your ferret has dry skin, spray him lightly with a mixture of 1 part lotion and 20 parts water. Dry with a towel; in fact, if you put the towel on the floor the ferret will probably have such fun rolling around in it that he will do the drying process alone.

You may want to finish the drying process (especially in the winter) with a hair dryer set on low. If your ferret is shedding (usually in spring or fall), a light brushing with a stiff hairbrush will help speed up the process. This is a good time to provide fresh bedding too. Then treat yourself by enjoying cuddling this sweet-smelling, soft-furred little pet.

Between baths you might try a "dry" bath. Lightly sprinkle the ferret with baby powder and rub it into the fur down to the skin. Gently brush to remove excess powder and loose hair.

Clipping back the ferret's nails once a month will prevent your pet from tripping if he gets caught up on carpeted surfaces and also prevent infection due to overgrowth. Extreme care should be exercised not to cut the red-colored section extending from the root of the nail. To see it, just hold the nail up to a bright light. Most ferrets will hate having their nails clipped. It's easier to sneak up on them while they are asleep or put a drop of a tasty vitamin supplement on their stomachs. They will be so busy licking it off they will forget what you are doing.

If you feel hesitant about clipping your ferret's nails, your veterinarian can do it and show you the proper procedure.

Ears can be cleaned with a cotton swab dipped in peroxide and used very gently. Ferrets' ears collect ear wax and removing the ear wax once a month will reduce the risk of bacteria build up. Clean the outer ear using the peroxide, then dry with a fresh swab. Repeat until no more dirt or wax is visible. Use the same procedure for the ear canal, cleaning with a very gentle twirling motion.

Plaque can form on the ferret's 40 teeth above and under the gumline, causing infection leading to kidney disease. Dry food will reduce the plaque formation. Check with your veterinarian to see if there is a large buildup of plaque. He or she will remove it while the ferret is sedated. After a professional cleaning you can brush the ferret's teeth with a soft child's toothbrush. This can be done two to three times a week.

Toys and Treats

Like most children, ferrets would like to exist entirely on treats. Of course, this is not possible, but there are many treats that can be offered without worry. Ferrets vary with their likes and dislikes of food. Ours enjoyed raisins and storebought ferret treats more than anything; we have heard from other members that they can't get their ferrets to touch them. Favored treats of many ferrets are

Although ferrets enjoy treats, they should be given in limited quantities. They will gorge themselves on snacks if allowed.

Always give your ferret a treat when returning him to the cage after playtime. Nutritious ferret snacks are available in pet stores.

cucumbers, cooked shrimp, baby food, vegetables and fruits, citrus fruits, and pieces of dry cereal. Other nutritious treats can be obtained through most veterinarians. Always give a treat to your pet when returning him to the cage after playtime (except if the ferret is being disciplined for biting).

Ferrets should **never** have dairy products, sweets such as candy or cake, or alcohol. All treats should be fed in very limited quantities; ferrets have small stomachs and will fill up on treats, ignoring their regular, more nutritious food. For that reason, limit treats to about two teaspoons daily.

Watch ferrets if you give them little scraps of food while they are running free—they will take it to their favorite hiding place. Check this place (or places) to be sure no decomposed food is hidden away.

Although ferrets will make up their own games, a wide variety of toys will add to their (and your) enjoyment of life. One favorite toy is flexible piping, such as the type used for dryer venting, with the wire ends covered with tape. Ferrets will spend much happy time running through the pipe, and when tired out, like to curl up in it for a nap.

We discourage use of soft rubber chew toys because the ferret can quickly shred them and ingest the small rubber pieces, which can cause intestinal blockage.

Crinkly plastic bags (not the smooth, clingy kind) are real favorites. Ferrets love the noise created by crumpling them up,

Ferrets love to play and can turn almost any household item into a toy. Ping-pong balls, paper bags, and empty boxes can provide hours of fun.

THE GUIDE TO OWNING A FERRET

wrestling and crawling in the bag. To prevent smothering, be sure to punch several holes in the bag.

Many happy playtimes are spent with a ferret chasing after a toy pulled on a string by you. (Let them "catch" it often enough for it to be fun for them). When playing alone, ferrets enjoy a hard rubber toy tied with a string to a door knob. They will spend much time pulling it and tugging it around. Take an empty egg carton or shoe box, attach a string and pull it around the room. They will love to chase it and might even climb aboard for a ride.

"Condos" (homemade or from a pet store) are fun and make good sleeping places. An old pair of blue jeans provides enjoyment when the ferrets run in and out of the legs.

Make a ferret wagon out of a small box or plastic basket with side openings, two dowels, and four margarine lids or wooden wheels. Tie string or rope to pull the wagon and one or more ferrets around, or have one chase the passenger.

One half of a plastic egg or pantyhose container is great fun. Place on a smooth floor, flat side down, and watch an endless game of ferret hockey as your pet tries vainly to pick it up in his teeth and paws but succeeds only in pushing it ever farther away.

Ferrets also enjoy cat scratching posts covered with carpet (especially those with toys on an attached spring).

Other fun toys are the tubes from paper towels; an empty egg crate with string attached to use as a pull toy; ping-pong balls; a small medicine bottle with a bell inside (be sure bottle is securely sealed); small cat toys made of hard rubber; an empty paper grocery bag; an empty aluminum pie pan to push around (makes a satisfying noise on a bare floor); large (9 by 12 or larger) used manila envelopes; dog squeaker toys of hard rubber only; and baby crib toys made of hard plastic.

When playtime is over, ferrets are great housekeepers—they will drag their prized possessions under a piece of furniture or into some secluded area.

Furry invented a game that could have been very profitable to us if we had let it continue. One evening a visitor opened her purse and left it on the floor. The next day when we were inspecting Furry's hiding place for hidden food scraps we found two five-dollar bills he had taken from our guest's purse! We were a bit red-faced as we returned the cash with explanations.

The Great Outdoors

Ferrets love the sociability and excitement of outdoor excursions and travel with you. There are a few things to be aware of before you take your ferret outside. One basic rule—always keep a collar on your pet, preferably with a small tag with your name and phone number. If there is room on the reverse side, list a friend or relative's name and number, in case you are not home if someone reports they have found your pet.

You've probably seen proud ferret owners walking with their pets on leashes. You can join them with a little advance preparation. Practice leash walking your ferret at home. Be sure your ferret is comfortable with the harness and can't wriggle out.

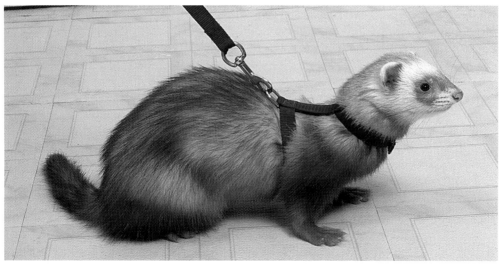

Many ferret owners train their pets to walk on a leash. If you take your pet outdoors, be sure that he wears a collar with an identification tag in case he becomes lost.

When outdoors, watch to see if your pet is nervous, frightened by traffic noise, humans, or other animals. If so, pick him up and come home. Some ferrets never adjust to outdoor exploration. **Never leave your ferret alone outside.** Large dogs, cats, or small children who think the ferret is a toy could attack and injure your pet.

In summer, sidewalks can be very hot and a ferret's paws can quickly burn. In winter if salt is used on the sidewalk or street to melt ice, never let your ferret walk on it. The salt will burn the ferret's paws.

Snow is great fun for ferrets to frolic in. Be sure you stay with them and let them play for no more than five minutes. When they are done, dry and warm them thoroughly.

Taking your ferret on a vacation is possible, and it is done quite often. To transport your ferret safely, use a carrying cage. Be sure the latches on the carrying case and cage are secure and make sure a collar with a name tag is worn by your pet at all times. Let him get accustomed to the cage by letting him sleep and eat in it for short intervals several days prior to the trip. If you are traveling out of state, get a health record including immunization history from your vet. Be sure your present address is listed. This will make it possible for you to take your ferret into states where they are illegal. Check with your veterinarian about a prescription for a sedative if your ferret is nervous in the car.

Although many ferrets enjoy going outdoors, never leave your ferret unattended outside. He could run away or get injured by another animal.

Because your ferret's food may not be available during travel, take along a supply of his regular diet. This is not the time to experiment with strange foods.

If you are flying, call as far ahead as possible to see if your pet can travel on your flight. Some airlines permit pets in the cabin in an approved pet carrier if no other passenger has a pet on the same flight. Other airlines will let your pet fly in the baggage compartment (check with your veterinarian to see if this method of travel is advised). A few airlines will not fly ferrets at all.

If you are planning a motor trip, be sure the temperature is comfortable (not above 80 degrees or lower than 55 degrees). Never leave your ferret unattended in the car and be sure no escape is possible through windows. Plan your route to stay at hotels, motels, or campgrounds that accept small pets. The FFC offers a listing of such facilities around the United States.

If you travel with your ferret in the summer, you must make sure he is cool. Travel in the early morning or late evening, if possible. If your car is air-conditioned be sure the air does not blow directly on the ferret's carrier. To ensure coolness, fill a plastic, watertight bottle (such as for soda or milk) three-quarters full, wrap in a towel, and place in carrier. The ferret can get near it or not as he chooses.

When arriving at a hotel or motel, remove your ferret from the carrying case to his regular cage (if possible). Since the hotel/motel room is not ferret-proofed, you could easily lose your pet when he explores.

One ferret owner reported the loss of her ferret in a motel. Her owners had thoroughly checked out the motel room and felt it was safe. In fact, during playtime the first evening, all was fine. The next morning, the ferret disappeared—nowhere to be found in the room.

Sassy, a one-year-old female, was very small. She had been seen going under the heating and air conditioning unit and coming out again; she was only hiding under the molding of the unit. Sassy's owners had not seen a small hole where the wiring went into the floor. That is where she went and was stuck between the floor of the room and the ceiling below. With endless corridors to travel, she became lost.

After the maintenance man tore the unit apart, her owners kept calling down the tiny hole for her. No sounds came back to confirm she was there. Some time later, using a flashlight, her owners saw some movement. The woman squeezed her hand into the opening and felt the ferret's nose, but the hole was too small to reach her and pull her out. In desperation, they took a toy (a cat teaser fishing pole) and dangled it in the hole. Sassy grabbed it right away and as she was being coaxed, she pulled herself up out of the hole, covered with soot. Although this story has a happy ending, little Sassy could have perished.

Ferret Health Care

As a responsible pet owner, you will, of course, want to provide your ferret with the best possible health care to ensure a long and healthy life. Susan A. Brown, DVM, recommends this preventive health care program for ferrets:

The initial veterinary examination should include a complete physical including an ear mite check, update on canine distemper vaccine if needed, a discussion of diet and general care, neutering of males and spaying of females

Ferrets should visit the veterinarian at least once a year for a checkup. The vet will check and clean your ferret's teeth to remove tartar.

if not done previously, a discussion of a hairball laxative to prevent hairballs or if foreign bodies have been ingested, and heartworm medicine if necessary in geographical area.

Annually, up to three years of age, a complete physical exam is necessary, including booster canine distemper vaccines and heartworm medication.

In ferrets three to seven years and older, there is an increased incidence of serious disease. Physical exams should be performed every six months. At least annually a complete blood chemistry and whole body X-ray should be performed. Other diagnostic tests should be administered as necessary, and tartar should be cleaned from teeth. Ferrets over seven years of age should have the diagnostic tests described above every six months.

CANINE DISTEMPER VACCINE

The first vaccination for this illness is given at eight weeks of age and again at three months. After that, annual inoculations are advised. Even if your ferret is not going to be exposed to a dog, he should still receive this vaccine, because the virus can be brought to your ferret on your clothing, shoes, or hands. If you don't know if your ferret has been vaccinated, it's recommended that you begin a schedule (with yearly boosters). Symptoms of canine distemper include a loss of appetite six to eight days after exposure to the virus. The corners of the eyes will show a discharge.

RABIES VACCINE

Until 1990, there was no approved vaccine against rabies for ferrets. Now vaccines are available. It is recommended that healthy ferrets three months or older receive an annual subcutaneous vaccination.

HEALTH PROBLEMS

Ferrets, like any other animal, are susceptible to certain types of health problems. We have searched our files and will present some of the most frequently reported problems and tips for avoiding many of them. Although this list looks alarming, we are not suggesting your ferret will have most—or any—of these problems. It is merely included to alert owners of potential problems that can be treated before they worsen.

Intestinal Tract Obstruction

This common, rapidly fatal condition is usually caused by swallowing foreign material such as rubber from soft pet toys, rubber from shoe soles, pencil erasers, protective tips from the bottom of chairs, hairballs, and bits of rubber bands. Symptoms of the blockage may not appear immediately. The material may spend days to months in the stomach where it will cause periodic blockage as it rolls around. As the stomach tries to push out the material, signs include lethargy with loss of appetite and vomiting. Stools may be small in amount, be black and sticky, or non-existent. When the material moves back into the stomach, the ferret will seem better and resume his appetite.

This may go on for weeks or months. When the material is pushed into the intestine there will probably be a complete blockage, and food and fluids will not be able to move through. This results in rapid dehydration of the body issues and fatal changes in the electrolyte balance. Death may occur within 24 to 48 hours. Symptoms at this point include severe depression, dull, lifeless looking eyes, bloating and tenderness of the abdominal area and vomiting. If any of these signs appear, go to the veterinarian immediately.

Hairballs

Use a hairball laxative for cats (available in pet stores). Give the ferret a one-inch squeeze of the laxative paste every two to three days. This pleasant tasting product will lubricate the hair as it accumulates and keep it moving out of the stomach.

Heat Stress/Heat Stroke

Ferrets become lethargic in temperatures over 80 degrees. If the temperature goes over 85 degrees, they are prone to heat exhaustion, which can be fatal. High humidity will increase the incidence of heat stroke. To prevent this problem, avoid trips in non-air-conditioned cars in hot weather. Never leave any pet in the car even on a relatively cool day, as the car heats up quickly. Provide a constant source of fresh drinking water. Keep cages in a shaded, area. Cages must be well ventilated. If your ferret shows signs of heat stress (panting, bright red gums, tongue hanging from mouth, signs of weakness, muscle tremors, lying perfectly flat or unconscious) take immediate steps; put the cage in a shaded, ventilated area, immerse the ferret in lukewarm (not cold) water, and contact a veterinarian immediately.

Ear Mites

If you notice frequent head shaking or scratching, rubbing of the ears on the floor, or crying, it could be the result of these parasites, which will also cause the ears to look dirty. Although this is not a serious problem and is easily treated by a veterinarian, it can cause severe suffering to your ferret.

Your ferret will shed in the spring and in the fall. Ferrets enjoy being groomed and regular brushing will prevent hairballs.

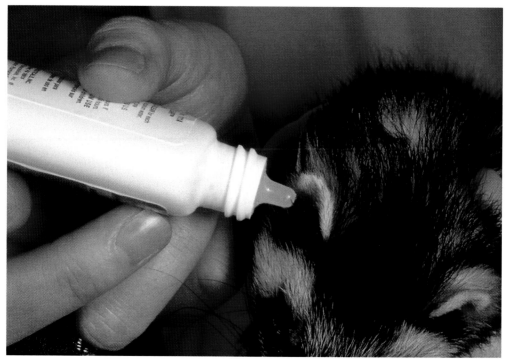

A ferret's ears should be kept clean. Your vet will check your pet for ear mites. If found, they are easy to treat.

Heartworm

Although this problem is mostly prevalent in the southeast US, these internal parasites have been spread by mosquitoes to almost every state. Adult heartworms live in the right side of the heart and arteries supplying blood to the lungs. Symptoms include weight loss, jaundice, and coughing. Prevention is the best approach. Discuss this problem with your veterinarian.

Ringworm

This problem is indicated by inflammations covering many parts of the body. The skin may become toughened and red with scaly crusts. Consult your veterinarian.

Scabies (*Sarcoptes Scabiei*)

Symptoms are swollen or scabby paws.

If your veterinarian diagnoses this as the problem, you must dispose of all bedding materials and thoroughly disinfect the cage.

Valley Fever (Coccidiosis)

This problem is caused by a fungus that produces spores that become airborne and cause infection when inhaled. Symptoms (alone or combined) are a chronic respiratory infection or cough, skin lesion, joint enlargement, loss of weight, loss of appetite, lethargy, and fever. This disease is treatable—consult your veterinarian.

Cardiomyopathy

This disease of the heart muscle is seen primarily in male ferrets over three years old. The muscle of the heart becomes thickened, causing it to pump less blood per beat, leading to poor circulation and, eventually, death. Symptoms include increased sleeping time, collapsing for short periods during play, lethargy, poor appetite, and difficulty awakening the ferret.

Cold and Flu

Ferrets are susceptible to the same types of cold and flu viruses that infect humans. It is very unlikely that a ferret would catch a human illness, but if anyone in your household has a cold or flu, avoid getting the ferret near the sufferer; wash hands before and after touching the ferret. If your ferret's symptoms last longer than two to three days, if appetite is poor or other symptoms surface, a visit to the veterinarian is in order.

Enteritis

Bloody stool and diarrhea, especially during warm weather, requires an immediate visit to the veterinarian. Symptoms of enteritis are intermittent diarrhea with normal food intake, as well as loss of weight.

Lymphosarcoma

This is a cancer of the lymphatic system, which is part of the body's immune system. Many animals exhibit no symptoms for a long period, and the disease is first diagnosed through blood tests. Noticeable symptoms include swollen lymph nodes, enlarged spleen, lethargy, poor appetite, labored breathing, diarrhea, or hind leg weakness.

Insulinoma

This pancreatic cancer is the most common one suffered by ferrets. The disease causes abnormally high levels of insulin to be produced, which causes sugar to be driven into the cells too rapidly. This causes a drop in the blood sugar level and the brain becomes sugar-starved, causing the ferret to behave in a strange way. The ferret will stare blankly for a few minutes, then return to normal. There may also be drooling or salivating, enlarged spleen, frantic pawing at the mouth, comatose behavior, and seizures. If your ferret develops seizures, you should administer honey and water by mouth until the pet is alert or seizures have stopped. Give his usual food or meat-type baby food to get protein in the body, and consult your veterinarian immediately.

Aleutian Disease

This is the result of an AIDS-like parvovirus that is able to survive on many surfaces and in most temperatures. It is spread through saliva, hair, handling, feces, milk, urine, and insects, especially flies. Symptoms include pneumonia, tarry stool, muscular wasting, hind quarter paralysis, extreme mastitis, lack of appetite, kidney failure, dribbling of urine, and lethargy. A blood test to specifically identify this virus is necessary.

Adenocarcinoma

This cancer of the adrenal glands is almost as common as insulinoma. Symptoms include hair loss over part or all of the body, dry and brittle coat; thinning of skin, lethargy, consumption of more drinking water, and more frequent urination. The skin may become intensely

The claws of a ferret should be trimmed on a regular basis. If you are unsure how to do this, the vet can show you. Never have your ferret declawed!

itchy with red patches, scaling and flaking. A pot-bellied appearance may occur.

Skin Tumors

These should be removed because they are usually irritating to the pet and may become malignant. If your ferret develops a mast cell tumor, which is a round, raised, itchy, button-like lump, or a sebaceous gland adenoma, which is wart-like and bleeds easily, consult your veterinarian about removal.

Scratching

There are many reasons for scratching. One is simply dry skin. If this is the cause,

cut back on baths, and be sure there is no dry heat blowing on ferrets. A humidifier is helpful in some cases.

Fleas

If fleas are suspected, treat the ferret himself. There are several good products on the market that are safe and effective. Your veterinarian may recommend one of the newer spot-on flea treatments available for dogs and cats. These work very well. Pump sprays also give an immediate flea-kill, but do not have long-term effects. Check with your vet to see what flea treatment he or she

THE GUIDE TO OWNING A FERRET

recommends. Flea combs work very well as ferrets usually learn to tolerate a few minutes of combing every other day or so.

Treat the environment. Be sure to use a product that is safe for ferrets and yet capable of killing the larval stage of the flea. The best products available for consumer use are foggers or sprays. These are available through a veterinarian. If you have your home sprayed professionally, use caution. Some of the new, granulated pesticides used by professionals can be highly toxic to ferrets, even though they carry no label warnings. Do not have your house treated with this compound if you have ferrets.

If you are in doubt about the safety or efficacy of a flea product, call your veterinarian.

Fleas also carry tapeworms, and ferrets are susceptible to them. If you notice small, white worms in your ferret's stool, this is what they will be.

Ticks

It is not likely that your ferret will have ticks unless he is out in grassy areas. When removing a tick, be sure to pull out the entire insect. If the head stays inside the ferret's skin, it can cause infection. Plucking is the best removal method. Clean the area with peroxide and watch the area for infection.

Lyme Disease

Since first diagnosed in the northeast in the 1960s, Lyme disease has been spreading. It is borne by a small tick that carries the disease-causing organism. Humans cannot contract the disease from infected animals—it is spread by tick bite only. However it has been spread from animal to animal through urine contact. Symptoms in pets include intermittent shifting lameness, swollen joints or joint pain, a persistent or recurrent fever with no apparent cause, loss of appetite, swollen lymph nodes, depression, and pain. Later stages of the disease produce neurological, kidney, and heart problems. To prevent Lyme disease, inspect your pet regularly when

If you are not home during the day, a second ferret to keep yours company may be a good idea.

in tick-infested areas. If ticks are found, remove them immediately.

Diarrhea

If your pet has more than two watery bowel movements or has black, green, or bloody diarrhea, call your veterinarian. One cause of diarrhea in ferrets is the organism *Campylobacter*, which is contagious to humans. Handle feces with a scoop and thoroughly wash your hands if your ferret has this problem.

Hair Loss

The loss of hair on the tail may range from slight to complete baldness with accompanying black spots on the tail, which are plugged hair follicles. While this problem usually corrects itself, it is best to consult your veterinarian to be sure that it is not due to a disease or nutritional deficiency.

If there are bald patches on other areas of the body, your pet may have adrenal gland disease. Be sure to get immediate medical attention for this problem.

Pawing at the Mouth

If accompanied by nausea, gagging, or vomiting, pawing at the mouth could indicate the presence of foreign bodies, such as shreds of rubber in the stomach. This can also be caused by gum inflammation. In pets over the age of three, it could indicate the presence of a tumor of the pancreas (insulinoma). Be sure to consult your veterinarian.

Always call your veterinarian immediately if your ferret:

1. Stops eating
2. Is lethargic
3. Is vomiting
4. Is choking or coughing
5. Develops diarrhea or bloody stools
6. Is scratching at ears continuously
7. Is drooling
8. Becomes suddenly more aggressive or passive
9. Has swelling or lumps on body
10. Emits strange odors from ears, anus, or mouth
11. Has an unusual discharge
12. Is losing an excessive amount of weight
13. Appears bloated or uncomfortable
14. Is breathing abnormally
15. Has nosebleeds
16. Develops loss of bladder or bowel control
17. Shows signs of weakness or confusion
18. Loses control in legs
19. Is shaking or rolling
20. Collapses
21. Shows blue gums or tongue

It is always better to be safe than to be sorry.

You know your pet and his daily routine best. If you notice any unexplained change of habits or disposition, have it checked out.

It is advisable to always keep an eye on food dishes (especially those shared by two or more ferrets). Be sure each ferret is eating what he normally consumes. Lack of appetite is often the first symptom of many problems.

If your veterinarian prescribes medicine, take the advice of one of our members. She had to dose her ferret on a

Ferrets are loyal, loving pets who deserve the best treatment you can provide for them.

daily basis over a long period of time and, although it was not a pleasant experience for her or her ferret, she developed the least traumatic way of administering the dosage.

1. Liquefy a pill in a small oral syringe rather than hiding it in food or trying to force it down the pet's throat.

2. Try to medicate the ferret when he is already awake, rather than forcing him to waken from a deep sleep.

3. Try to administer the medicine at the same time each day.

4. It's best to give oral medicine when the ferret has some food in his stomach, unless this is not advised by your veterinarian. If given on an empty stomach it may be vomited up.

5. If more than one kind of medicine is given, try to do all the medicating at the same time. If possible, mix all the medications together. However, consult your vet before doing this.

6. Wear a full apron or protective smock to prevent damage to clothing.

7. Hold the ferret in your lap with your left arm, slide syringe into side of ferret's mouth, and push the plunger in quickly.

8. Try not to allow syringe to touch the whiskers. This seems to alert the ferret that medicine is on the way and causes struggling.

9. Follow the medicine with a good-tasting treat and then play with your pet. This will make him forget the unpleasant experience.

Do not use medicine that was prescribed for another ferret or medicine that is on hand from a previous illness. Continue the dosage prescribed by the veterinarian—do not stop the medication just because the symptoms disappear.

Breeding

Breeding ferrets is a matter to be considered seriously. It is not easy for an "amateur"—many things can go wrong. The jill may be physically unable to bear kits or she may prove to be a bad mother, refusing to nurse the kits, or even attacking and killing them. If she is unable to nurse her young, they will starve to death unless a surrogate mother can be found. You may be able to nurse the kits on a nursing formula, but it is doubtful the entire litter will survive.

Another problem you will face is the "adoption" of the kits. Can you be sure they will be placed in loving homes? Or will they be bought as a novelty and ignored once the newness has worn off? Besides the initial cost of the ferret, prospective owners should be informed about maintenance costs (physical exams,

If you are not going to breed your ferret, have it spayed or neutered. It will keep your pet healthier and more docile.

These baby ferrets are two days old. Kits are born hairless and are about one-and-a-half inches long.

inoculations, etc). Will you be willing and able to spend time with the new owners instructing them on proper ferret care?

For these reasons, we strongly urge neutering and spaying of all ferrets unless they are owned by professional breeders. Neutering and spaying also makes males more docile and both sexes sweeter-smelling.

If you have made your decision not to breed, be sure to have your jill spayed. If she goes into heat (estrus) and is not bred, she will develop aplastic anemia, a fatal condition. If she has already gone into heat, she still need not be bred. An injection of 100 units of a substance called HCG will bring 90 percent of female ferrets out of heat in two to three weeks, after which time they can be spayed. This is a safe, effective alternative to breeding to end estrus.

If you decide to breed, we encourage you to have your jill examined by your veterinarian prior to breeding.

Females reach sexual maturity at four to five months of age and have breeding periods twice a year, normally in the spring and fall. However, artificial lighting will affect the time of estrus and a female housed indoors may go into heat at other times. Estrus is easy to detect because it causes the vulva to swell. Other signs of heat are increased body odor, wet rear legs, and lack of appetite.

The best choice for a stud should be over one year old and definitely no

This young ferret is about 16 days old. Its eyes will open at about five weeks of age.

younger than nine months old. Do not breed father/daughter, brother/sister, or mother/son. This inbreeding is too close and is likely to produce defective kits. Because it is imperative that the female be bred shortly after going into heat, line up prospective studs early. Veterinarians may be able to help you.

Females should be bred on the tenth day of their heat cycle. Breeding is a very violent procedure. The male will bite the back of the female's neck and drag her around the cage until she submits. Most females will fight back, with accompanying screams and hisses. Although this is frightening to witness, it is part of their mating rite and not a problem. However, if she bites furiously and discharges large amounts of anal gland secretions, she is not ready. A receptive female will relax in the grip of the mate, close her eyes, and go limp. If the stud is rejected by the jill, remove him and try again in a few days. Meanwhile, let the jill sleep with a cloth

taken from the stud's cage so she will be more receptive in the future.

After breeding has occurred, check the female to be sure she has not developed any vaginal infections. If there is a colored discharge from the vulva, she should be treated by your veterinarian with antibiotics.

The male and female should be left together for 48 hours. Copulation will occur many times. Between matings, they will share their bed and food amicably. Once the breeding act has been completed, the vulva will return to normal size within 24 to 48 hours. Not all matings produce young.

Gestation period is approximately 42 days. About a week or ten days before her due date, provide your jill with a nest box (a plastic dishpan is fine) containing a small bath towel. The nest box should be in a quiet area. Be sure the towel is not too large, or the tiny kits may become lost in it.

The jill will lose quite a bit of hair about a week before she gives birth. This is normal and nothing to be concerned about. Her nipples will enlarge and the urogenital area will become darker purple and more turgid. The jill will spend more time sleeping prior to birth.

On the day the birth is to take place the jill will become quieter, lose interest in food, and won't want to leave her cage to play.

The normal birth process will take approximately two hours. Litters range in size from six to twelve. Kits are usually born in a sequence of pairs, with a few minutes rest between pairs. Kits are born hairless, with their eyes closed, and are almost transparent. They are about one-and-a-half inches in length.

Usually, the jill will take care of the birthing process herself, cutting the umbilical cords, ingesting the afterbirth, and cleaning the kits.

If an hour passes without productive labor, or the jill becomes glassy-eyed and weak, there is a problem and the veterinarian should be consulted immediately.

Although most jills produce milk immediately, a few do not for 12-14 hours. This is a serious problem for the kits, who must be fed by a surrogate mother or fed using a formula. For this reason it is necessary to have a surrogate mother available and a supply of formula and infant nursing bottles available. Hand feeding is very difficult and requires round-the-clock attention.

Not all jills are good mothers—some will refuse to nurse their kits and some will attempt to eat them. It is important that you closely monitor the situation.

Baby ferrets can be weaned by soaking dry food in water. They can be adopted out to new homes at six weeks of age or older.

Usually if a jill is a poor mother the first time there is not much hope that she will improve in the future. It is best to spay this jill before a second estrus.

Do not disturb the jill with her kits for the first 48 hours. Then look for any dead kits that should be removed. Do not clean the nest box for three weeks.

Occasionally eye infections may develop before the eyes are open. This is signaled by swelling. Be sure to contact your veterinarian immediately if this happens.

Between five and six weeks of age the kits will open their eyes. At this time they may be weaned. It is best to wean by taking the largest kits from their mother. This will permit the milk to dry up gradually. To wean, place a shallow bowl of warm milk in the cage and hold the kits to it until they begin to drink. Drinking can be encouraged by placing a few drops on your palm and putting it against their mouths. Kits are introduced to food by soaking dry feed with water.

It is vital to have physical contact with the kits daily from the age of three weeks. This will domesticate them and accustom them to humans. The more they are gently handled, the better pets they will become.

At the age of six weeks or older the kits may be adopted out to other homes. We strongly urge you to be sure that the kits will be loved and wanted by their new owners. If you are keeping one or more of the kits, separate them from their mother so they can become socialized and interact with humans.

It is wise to charge a fee to buy the kits. By charging for the kits, you are ensuring the new owners are serious about having a ferret and will value it. Many sellers include a book on ferret care with the kit.

Many of our members require the individuals adopting kits to fill out the following Pet Pride Promise in duplicate. One copy is given to the new owners and the other retained by the sellers.

PET PRIDE PROMISE

1. I fully realize my responsibility as I accept this ferret called (name of ferret) from (name of owner) on (date).
2. I will keep this ferret with me as long as it lives unless extreme circumstances prevent, in which event I will procure suitable placement.
3. I will devote a reasonable time for daily companionship with this ferret.
4. I will make proper provision for this ferret in the case of any personal extreme emergency.
5. I agree to follow instructions as to its care, its housing, its food, its treatment, and its health.
6. I agree to study a good ferret care manual and to follow its instructions.
1.) Birthdate of ferret
2.) Sire
3.) Dam
4.) Owner
Purchased from (name, address, telephone number)
Signature of owner

Ferret Owners' Concerns

We receive many letters from our members on a variety of subjects. We are going to try to address some of the most common concerns.

TWO OR MORE FERRETS?

Our members frequently ask if they should consider getting a "friend" for their single ferret. Generally, it is a wonderful idea, and after an introduction period the two usually become inseparable. They will be company and playmates for each other, providing many happy hours of companionship for themselves while you are away.

At first, the new ferret and the old may not get along. One member reported it took almost one year for her ferrets to become friendly. When she adopted a two-year-old female (spayed and descented) ferret from the Humane Society and introduced her to her one-year-old female

Small animals such as ferrets need a lot of rest during the day. They will sleep for hours when the owner is gone.

(also spayed and descented), the new ferret attacked her immediately. After several weeks of constant attacking by the older ferret, our member was advised by the veterinarian to let them fight it out. She was reluctant to do that.

For one year, the ferrets were separated at all times even though they would bite and claw the cages to get to each other.

Our member felt guilty that she had brought an intruder into the house to upset her younger ferret's life. She also refused to take the older ferret back to the Humane Society since she had made a commitment to care for her.

One day, the ferrets were accidentally out of the cages at the same time. As usual, the older ferret attacked, but this time the younger one refused to accept any more abuse and attacked in return. The older ferret backed off immediately. After several months our member lost the fear that the older one would attack the younger. Now these ferrets get along well. There are times when the older one gets a bit rough, but it's nothing serious. Basically, they work it out themselves.

Don't ever let ferrets fight to the point of serious bodily harm. Try to let them out together and be with them constantly to watch for serious aggression. When they attack, push the attacker away and say, "NO!" firmly. Ferrets do have the ability to learn what "No," means, but they don't always obey. When you have them out together, make sure you are in a room where they can't get under the furniture.

If that happens, you won't be in control of the situation. Never strike or scare the ferrets.

There are a few negatives to having two ferrets. If your ferret has bad habits, they probably will be picked up by the new addition.

You should consider if you will have time, space, money, and love enough for a second ferret. One thing you don't have to worry about is losing your pet's love to a new ferret. Your ferrets will always love you as only an owner can be loved—the affection they have for other ferrets will not diminish theirs for you.

LEAVING YOUR FERRET ALONE

Do you feel guilty or anxious about leaving your ferret alone at home? You shouldn't. Usually when a ferret has no one to play with, he will curl up for a nice long nap. Be sure that when you leave, he has plenty of food, water, a cozy place to sleep, and a toy or two.

If you are planning to be away from home more than overnight and can't take your ferret with you, you will have to provide good care while you are gone. If your pet is to be taken to a boarding facility, check it out well. Is it clean and odor-free? Is the staff friendly and attentive to the animals? Will you be permitted to provide your ferret's favorite food in order to prevent feeding problems? If the facility is not affiliated with a veterinarian, be sure to leave the name of your veterinarian and take along a copy of the ferret's medical records.

Ferrets can be a handful, but their love, affection, and loyalty to the owner is worth the time.

If you are keeping your pet at home, be sure to have someone come in at least once a day to check on him, empty the litter pan, and provide food, fresh water, and companionship. The ferret should not have the run of the house. It's better to confine the pet to the cage or one room that has been ferret-proofed. Be sure there is proper ventilation.

Tell your "sitter" the signs of illness in a ferret.

It's a good idea to leave a book on ferret care for reference. Leave the name, address, and phone number of your veterinarian and a copy of the ferret's medical records.

We do urge you to consider this: although you may plan to be away from home for only a few hours, you might be prevented from returning home when you had planned due to bad weather, car trouble, ill health, or accident. If something comes up to prevent you from coming home for many hours or even days, make plans ahead for ferret care.

It's a good idea to give a key to a trusted neighbor who has been instructed on ferret care and knows who to contact in an emergency. Because ferrets are so small, it takes little time for them to dehydrate or become extremely hungry.

Pre-planned pet care is advisable. In the event of severe illness or death of owners, pets will need food, shelter, and attention from the very first day. Designate someone you trust to take immediate—if only temporary—custody of them. Provide written authorization for this caretaker; if appropriate, include a small check to cover short-term expenses. You probably have already given someone you trust an extra key to your home. Be sure whoever is designated to take your animals knows how to reach that person.

Post the pet caretaker's name, address, and phone number prominently in your home so those who might appear on the scene in an emergency can't miss it. Place this information in your wallet in case of an emergency. Give your attorney this information, too.

Long-term custody of pets may require more planning. It is wise to make a provision in your will for your pets. If no plans are made for them they may be taken to a pound.

The ideal solution is to line up a future home with someone you and your pets already know. However, if this is not possible, most pets will make the transition fairly well. You may direct your executor to use every possible means to find a home for them. You can also leave funds with a consenting individual with the request they care for your pet.

GENERAL MISBEHAVIOR

Although ferrets are very lovable, when they misbehave it seems they are plotting to annoy us deliberately. This is not the case. Your pet may not know he or she is doing something wrong. If that is the case, it is necessary to inform your ferret that he or she has some bad habits. The key to this is consistency. Whenever your ferret engages in misbehavior, correct him or her.

Ferrets are loveable, curious pets that like to explore.

One good method is to give a quick squirt with water from a plant sprayer. This isn't harmful, but the pet won't like it. If possible, remove the ferret from the area where he or she is misbehaving. A gentle tap with the finger on the ferret's nose and a loud and firm, "no" also works well. Never give your pet a treat or playtime sooner than ten minutes after the misbehavior.

There are many reasons for misbehavior: fear, loneliness, boredom, and illness are some. When frightened, some ferrets will hide under their blankets. Others will misbehave in response to fear.

If your pet is misbehaving while ill, this is understandable, and, if possible, permit the pet to do as he or she wishes. In most cases as soon as the pet is feeling better, the misbehavior will stop.

If you notice your ferret misbehaves when left alone, try to put him or her in an area where there isn't much to get into, or place him in the cage. If your pet constantly knocks over an item in his reach, you may want to move the item.

Be sure your pet has enough space to exercise. Play uses a lot of ferret energy and leaves less pep for misdeeds.

CLAWED CARPET

Ferrets love to scratch on interesting surfaces, which include carpet. To prevent this, spray the area with a biting deterrent. If the area clawed is at a seam (the end of a room, for instance), install a small metal plate used for carpet ends. This should prevent ruined carpeting.

Never have your ferret declawed.

LOST FERRETS

Since ferrets are so quick and small, it is no wonder they get lost. We advise you to

Be sure to watch your pet to see that it does not get into trouble. Never give your pet a treat after misbehavior.

take every measure to prevent their loss. Keep windows closed or securely screened in areas where ferrets roam. Even though the areas have been ferret-proofed, be sure the ferret does not slip out a door into a part of the house that has not been protected, or even outdoors. Be sure there are no holes in the walls, however tiny. Many ferrets have disappeared into walls of their homes and some people have had to tear out parts of the walls to recover their pets!

Check trash cans before disposing of the contents. Ferrets can climb easily into a trash can and if large plastic bags are used, that is a real attraction for them. Mail slots have also been used as an escape route for ferrets. Warn guests that your ferrets are able to get through doors quickly, and urge them to be sure they don't accidentally let your pet escape.

Most (if not all) ferrets are attracted by the sound of dog squeaker toys and will respond instantly to them. Start training them while they are young by squeaking the toy and when they come running give a treat as a reward. One day, you may be very happy that you started this training.

If you can't find your ferret and think he might have escaped outside, don't waste any time in starting the search. Ferrets are not able to exist very long without food and water and are easy prey for large animals. To attract your ferret, place his bed outside the house by the door along with food and water. Walk around the house or area where you believe your pet is, in ever-widening circles, calling your ferret's name and using the squeaker toy. It will help to have a picture that can be duplicated and posted on street signs. Mail delivery persons have also been very helpful in bringing ferrets back to their owners. Be sure all neighbors know what your ferret looks like.

We introduced our ferrets to our neighborhood children in an unusual and "fun" way. When we moved to a new home the neighborhood children bombarded us with questions about Furry and Heather: "What are they? Do they bite? Can I take them for a walk? Do they bark? Can they lick my ice cream cone?" When one of the children asked how old Furry was, the idea came to us to celebrate with a birthday party for him. He and Heather dined on raisins and ferret treats while the human guests enjoyed ice cream, cake, and soda. Since the guest of honor had fallen asleep before the guests left, a new way to express appreciation was derived by one of the boys. He simply reached in Furry's little house and shook his tail.

One ferret owner we know always let her ferrets run loose in the house for the entire night. One day, although it was winter, the temperature was mild, and she had absentmindedly left the sliding glass door open about five inches. The screen had not yet been installed for the season.

Children enjoy playing with ferrets and can help in training the animals.

As ferrets age, they require more sleep. An older ferret should receive a checkup twice a year.

The next morning the owner got up to let the dog out and found the door open. One ferret, Jill, was in the dining room eying the door, but since the cat was sitting on the other side of the door, Jill wouldn't venture out. However, Hobbit, who is not afraid of the cat, was gone.

A flashlight search around the house revealed nothing. The desperate owner called the police. Fifteen minutes later they called back, saying someone had reported finding a ferret.

Hobbit had ventured at least half a mile through woods and across a main road to someone's rabbit cage, where two rabbits were killed. When he broke into the cage, the rest of the rabbits got loose. The owner of the rabbits called the police to get Hobbit out of the cage. The owner of the rabbits and the dog catcher were afraid to touch Hobbit, and finally a pole was used to catch him.

Don't forget—if you have lost or found a ferret call your local animal shelter or police. A ferret club may also be able to help bring about a reunion.

OLDER FERRETS

Ferrets are considered "senior citizens" at about the age of five (earlier or later in individual cases). Healthy, older ferrets stay playful and energetic, in most cases, through middle and old age. However, there are a few changes owners will notice. To be sure they have the best quality "golden years," you might try some of these tips.

As ferrets age, they require more sleep. Be sure they are able to rest as much as they want and provide a cozy, draft-free place for them to sleep. Your ferret will still enjoy playtime with you. He or she will let you know when it's time to play. Your pet will continue to thrive on love and companionship and a nap or a rest on your lap is pleasurable for both ferret and owner.

As middle to old age approaches, ferrets' coats may not be as full or luxuriant in the winter. As long as there are no bald spots or heavy shedding, this is normal. A drop of a vitamin supplement is advised.

Because the pads of their feet may tend to become dry, a dab of petroleum jelly will help. If the ferret's hair seems to be more dry and rough, cut baths down to every six weeks or so. Pet shops will have products to be used on their coats.

If poor control of bladder or bowels occurs, have litter pans or beds easily

Responsible owners make sure that their ferrets have all the love and affection they deserve.

accessible. Sometimes weakness of hind legs (another problem associated with aging) makes it hard for your pet to enter and exit the litter pan. Be sure it is low enough for easy use.

Check your ferret's food dish. If age has caused tooth or gum problems, he may have trouble eating dry food.

If possible, keep your ferret's bed, food dish, and toys in the same place. Ferrets are creatures of habit and routine is comforting.

Consult with your veterinarian on special care for older ferrets. The vet will advise you on special diets or treatments needed.

If the time comes when your pet is too old or too ill to enjoy life, we strongly urge you to consult your veterinarian about available options. In some cases, the vet may recommend euthanasia.

When Furry was no longer able to enjoy life I was faced with this decision and it was one of the hardest things I've ever had to do. I asked my veterinarian to give him the injection and held Furry in my arms as he drifted peacefully off to sleep. We at the FFC firmly believe if your ferret is suffering and will not be able to recover to enjoy life, painless euthanasia is the final act of love you can perform for your ferret.

Dr. Jerry Rosseau, a psychotherapist, made a presentation at the Ferret Care Conference sponsored by the Association for Advancement of the Human Animal Bond. In his presentation he said, "When you open up your heart to allow yourself to be close to a ferret, you also open yourself up to feeling a sense of loss when that ferret dies. When watching ferrets dance merrily about it seems they will live forever. However, those involved with ferrets will eventually experience the loss of one of these endearing creatures."

Dr. Rosseau discussed stages of the grieving process. As you confront the death of a ferret you will experience a number of different stages of grief.

1. The first stage is shock and disbelief. There is a numbness that comes over us. This feeling is important for it will help us make the initial adjustment to the loss.

2. The second stage is anger. This stage is the hardest for people to handle. Sometimes we try to blame ourselves for our ferret's death. We become angry because we do not want to deal with this experience. We need to acknowledge and accept these feelings.

3. The third stage is sadness. It encompasses all the things we are going to miss. Sadness must be experienced. Talk to other ferret owners—share your sadness.

4. Acceptance of the loss is the next stage. It may take some time to get over the loss of your pet, but in time you will be able to move on with the rest of your life.

Ten Golden Rules of Responsible Ferret Care

1. I will have my ferret spayed or neutered as soon as my veterinarian determines it is safe to do so or will be responsible about breeding and adoption of kits.

2. I will give my ferret annual vaccinations, a veterinary checkup, and provide whatever medical care is required.

3. I will not let my ferret run loose outside without a harness and leash and will provide constant supervision.

4. I will feed my ferret only the best quality high-protein, low-ash food and give him plenty of fresh water to drink.

5. I will not leave my ferret unattended with infants or small children.

6. I will provide suitable, clean housing and sleeping quarters for my ferret.

7. I will let my ferret out if his cage every day for play and exercise.

8. I will handle my pet gently and always treat him with respect and affection.

9. I will make sure my home is safe for my ferret and make certain that he cannot escape from my home or get into places where injury could occur.

10. If I cannot keep my ferret, I will find him a suitable home or adoption center and not release him outdoors.

FERRET FANCIERS CLUB

Throughout the book, there have been several references to the Ferret Fanciers Club. My late husband Jay and I began this club in 1985 with a few members in Pittsburgh. As word spread, membership increased to our present number of more than 3,000 members around the world. We are a non-profit organization.

It seems appropriate to have Daniel (Dan) Huber, our Membership Director, tell you about the club and describe some of our services and activities:

"Since I became Membership Director in 1991, I have had the pleasure of speaking with many present and potential members, and I am struck by one thing all callers have in common—a sincere love of ferrets. Our membership includes owners, potential owners, health care professionals/educators, manufacturers of ferret foods, medicines, and related products and breeders.

We publish the *International Ferret Review* (IFR) six times a year, which is sent to all members. The IFR serves as a networking tool—our members are able to write in with questions or problems they are having and our readers are most cooperative by informing us of how they might have solved similar problems. Also the IFR keeps its readers up-to-date on any ferret news. We operate a 24-hour "Ferret Hotline" to answer emergency questions and act as a lost and found clearance.

In addition, we offer a large list of literature on ferrets, have a directory of veterinarians who specialize in ferret care, and inform our members of hotels, motels, and campgrounds that accept small pets. Our catalog offers treats and accessories for your ferret as well as owner-usable ferret related items. The FFC works to promote welfare of ferrets and to educate the public about them. One of our largest activities is providing copies of our newsletter to public libraries around the country.

A very important service we offer is ferret registration. To register your ferret, request a registration form. You will then simply submit a choice of three names (in order of preference), sex of the ferret,

With a good diet and proper care, your ferret will live a long, healthy life.

Ferrets are one of the world's fastest-growing pets. Many ferret clubs and organizations now exist.

Well-trained, properly cared-for ferrets make excellent pets.

coloration and, if known, date of birth and sire and dam's names with a small registration fee. We will check our files to prevent duplication of names and issue a record of registration. The registration will become part of the FFC permanent records. Registration is useful not only to permanently identify your pet but to help the FFC in its efforts to change legislation affecting ferrets. It is the most accurate method of determining the number of domestic ferrets there are and the number of people who own them. It was largely due to ferret registration records that manufacturers could be induced to develop a rabies vaccine.

Since ferrets are still not legal in all 50 states, we take an active role in urging their legalization. We are happy to work with our members in promoting "write 'n' fight" campaigns and inform our members as laws change.

We are very fortunate to have member veterinarians who will consult with other veterinarians in difficult cases. Their generosity in sharing experiences with unusual ferret-related problems has saved the lives of many ferrets.

Before I started as Membership Director, the FFC worked with other organizations to promote the development of a rabies vaccine. Presently Imrab is available for this purpose, and we are hopeful this availability will help us in our fight to legalize ferrets throughout the United States.

We look forward to hearing from our ferret friends at any time—the FFC mailbox is always filled with interesting, funny, and sometimes sad letters that Mary and I enjoy.

The FFC does not limit its help to members—we are glad to help anyone with a ferret-related problem. Don't forget—the purpose of the FFC is to help make life better for ferrets everywhere.

If you would like information on joining the FFC or need help with a problem, don't hesitate to contact us. Our mailing list is never sold or given out. We will never confirm if a certain individual is a member or use names in any publication without written permission.

To contact us, write: Ferret Fanciers Club, 711 Chautauqua Court, Pittsburgh, PA 15214 or call (412) 322-1161.

Index

Photo Credits

Joan Balzarini: p. 33
Isabelle Francais: front and back covers, pp. 1, 3, 5, 11-13, 15, 16, 19-20, 23, 25-26, 28-30, 32, 35, 37, 41, 44-45, 49, 51, 53-57, 60-62
Michael Gilroy: pp. 21, 46
Robert Pearcy: pp. 7, 9, 43
Lara Stern: p. 4
John Tyson: pp. 38, 40, 47